Artistry in Chip Carving
A Lyrical Style

Craig Vandall Stevens

Text written with and photography by Douglas Congdon-Martin

With illustrated,
step-by-step
instructions

Schiffer Publishing Ltd

77 Lower Valley Road, Atglen, PA 19310

Library of Congress Cataloging-in-Publication Data

Vandall Stevens, Craig.
    Artistry in chip carving : a lyrical style / Craig Vandall Stevens ;
text written with and photography by Douglas Congdon-Martin.
      p. cm. -- (A Schiffer book for woodcarvers)
    ISBN 0-88740-940-7 (paper)
    1. Wood-carving 2. Wood-carving--Patterns. I. Congdon-
Martin, Douglas. II. Title. III. Series.
TT199.7.V34 1996
736'.4--dc20   95-53835
                                                  CIP

Printed in Hong Kong
ISBN: 0-88740-940-7

Published by Schiffer Publishing Ltd.
77 Lower Valley Road
Atglen, PA 19310
Please write for a free catalog.
This book may be purchased from the publisher.
Please include $2.95 for shipping.
Try your bookstore first.

We are interested in hearing from authors
with book ideas on related subjects.

Contents

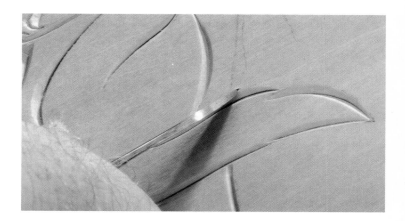

This book is most lovingly dedicated to Caroline,
who gently inspires me to reach a little higher.

Acknowledgments

I would like to acknowledge the staff at the College of the Redwoods Fine Woodworking Program, Jim Krenov, Michael Burns, David Welter, and Jim Budlong, who each encouraged my desire to continue refining my style of chip carving and explore the relationship between fine woodworking and chip carving. I would like to thank Wayne Barton for his over-my-shoulder suggestions and advice early on. I also would like to thank Marge Galloway for allowing me to borrow her very organized mind and for her help in reminding me "i before e except after c" or something like that. Special appreciation to my family and friends for their understanding that following the path of the heart is more important than following the path of convenience (in other words, never asking when I'm going to get a "real job").

I also would like to thank the nice folks at Schiffer Publishing for taking an interest in my work, especially Doug Congdon-Martin for making this project so much fun.

Lastly, to my two shopmates Willowby and Sidney, both truly wonder dogs!

Introduction

Several years ago I saw a simple repeated pattern carved down the legs of a small table. The idea that such a small, subtle detail could add so much interest to the piece of furniture germinated my interest in chip carving. I realized that the carving, which was barely noticeable across the room, had drawn me to look more closely. The idea of inviting someone to explore an object more intimately, whether with a carving, marquetry, or other interesting choices one makes, is an aspect of woodworking that holds a tremendous amount of appeal for me. This is part of what my (furniture making) teacher, Jim Krenov calls "the fingerprints of the craftsman."

Chip carving has allowed me to put into use a lifelong interest in drawing and sketching. I feel that this has benefitted my carving, and likewise the desire to carve interesting designs has probably enhanced my ability to draw because the drawing has a purpose. Many of my carving students have expressed hesitancy or intimidation at the idea of working on their own designs, stating an inability to draw as the reason. I encourage the reader, as I do my students, at least to give it an occasional try. (You can always hide those first few sketches in the bottom of a drawer or somewhere else never to be found by anyone else!) Like carving, drawing improves with practice and can become a very satisfying aspect of chip carving. If you have little or no experience at drawing but would like to learn more, you might look into cultural arts centers or adult education programs. As you will see on the following pages, the designs included here are inspired by nature.

Oriental brush painting, too, is inspired by nature, and has been a source of inspiration for me. The master brush painters of Japan and China are able to capture the grace of nature in their paintings with a minimum of brush strokes, often allowing the eye of the viewer to "complete" the suggestion of movement in the work. The style that has evolved in my own chip carving is an attempt to capture the simple but graceful lines of the natural world. I hope to convey a degree of the brush painter's sensitivity through the flow and movement of a few lines.

The initial drawing creates the foundation of each carving. After transferring the sketch to the wood, the actual carving begins. Because this approach to design requires the blending of two disciplines, I often find that the knife leads me in a direction different from my original drawing. In the process of working within this free flowing style, I've come to view chip carving as an opportunity to "compose" directly from the point of the knife, allowing the combined effort of hand, eye, and knife to create the carved image.

In this book I will discuss the technique of chip carving including the tools and their care, sharpening, wood selection, as well as design and transferring the drawing to the wood. I will take a project from the artwork, through the carving and finishing of the work

I wish you luck in exploring this style of chip carving and hope you enjoy the adventure.

SOME SUGGESTIONS

☞ When working on a small piece, use a larger lap size piece of wood below the workpiece to give some support and lessen the chance of slipping and cutting yourself.

☞ Secure your workpiece when working on harder woods or larger pieces.

☞ Work on your lap when possible. The distance to your lap is just right to help in keeping your elbow at your side.

☞ Wear a bandaid on your thumb to prevent your thumbnail from scratching or damaging the work surface.

☞ Use an index card to cover delicate, intricately carved work as you near completion. The card is easily repositioned for each cut to protect what you've already carved.

☞ The hand holding the workpiece is most likely to be cut in case of a slip. Develop the habit of holding the work above the knife so that it's not in the path of the blade.

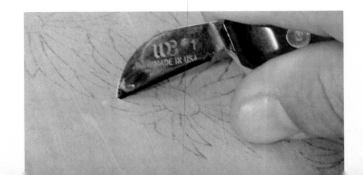

Wood Preparation

At many hardwood stores, you will find wood that has already been surfaced by a planer, but still needs some work before carving can begin. You can further refine the surface of the wood using a hand plane, cabinet scraper, or sandpaper. When sanding, use medium to fine grit paper wrapped around a cork-faced wooden block. I generally start with 180 or 220 grit and work up to 320 to 400 grit, sanding with the grain and using straight strokes. This leaves a nice, smooth finish, ready to lay out the carving design. Dust off the surface with a rag so there are no abrasive particles remaining to dull the knife.

What Wood Should I Use?

Suggested Woods

Common woods:
   Basswood
   Butternut
   Walnut
   White Pine
   Poplar
   Mahogany

Uncommon woods:
   European (Swiss) Pear
   Sugar pine
   Alaskan Yellow Cedar
   Port Orford Cedar
   Nutmeg
   Buckeye

I consider four things when I choose woods.

1. Hardness: The wood has to be soft enough that it can be carved using only the strength of your hand, but not so soft that it crushes under the cutting the edge of the knife.

2. Color: Lighter colors show off the contrast between the shadow and light better than darker woods.

3. Close, fine grain: Close grains hold detail very well, resulting in a nice crisp look to the carving.

4. Pattern of the grain: Some woods, like butternut, have distinct growth grain patterns. It may be beautiful, but it competes for attention when looking at a carving. More subtle grain patterns as in basswood and pear help the carving standout.

I must admit that I don't always follow these guidelines. For instance, my favorite wood to use in carving is swiss pear, but it is quite hard and I've had to build up the hand strength to carve it. Since I often use chip carving in the furniture I make, I sacrifice ease of carving for the beauty and strength.

A word about **Lesser Known Species.** Over the past few years many new wood have begun to become available to woodworkers and carvers. Some of these woods are suitable for chip carving and are certainly worth exploring. Many of these are ecologically harvested species from well-managed resources and available through specialized suppliers.

Two lesser known species that offer chip carving possibilities are:

Narra, a golden-brown wood from Papa New Guinea

Chokte kok, a deep red wood from the Yukatan Peninsula

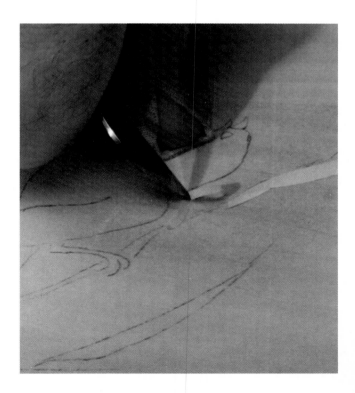

Sharpening

The carving knife (Number one) is the workhorse of chip carving and requires the most preparation. The two goals in sharpening are to keep a perfectly straight cutting edge and to reduce the angle of the bevel. This takes metal off the shoulder behind the cutting edge, reducing drag in the wood and increasing the maneuverability of the knife as you carve.

I use two, small ceramic sharpening stones for my carving knives. The darker is a medium , fast cutting grit and the white stone is considered super fine. Because they are made from a very hard, synthetic material, they stay perfectly flat. Other stones are usually softer and begin to dish-out with use. The problem is that the shape of the stone is transferred to the cutting edge of the knife, so a dished-out sharpening surface gives you a curved cutting edge.

Ceramic stones need no lubricant, making them cleaner and very portable. They are good, lifetime tools that I highly recommend.

Sharpening time for me is a creative time which allows me to begin to focus my attention on my carving. Not only does it prepare the knives for use, it also sharpens my mind and prepares me for the work ahead.

The first sharpening of the knife will be time consuming. People in my carving class often spend their entire first evening preparing their knife. The initial sharpening is on the medium stone. The ideal angle is 10 degrees. Wayne Barton has given the best suggestion for determining that angle. Simple lay a dime under the back edge of the blade and try to consistently sharpen at that angle.

Carving knife held on the sharpening stone with the back edge raised to a 10 degree angle (approximately the thickness of a dime).

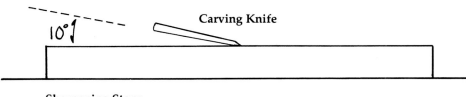

Sharpening Stone

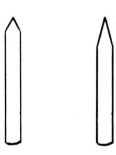

The bevel of a new knife sharpening (**left**) has a steep angle with thick shoulders just behind the cutting edge. Correctly sharpened (**right**), the angle has been reduced to about 10 degrees and the shoulder is less prominent.

After a number of strokes on one side, flip the blade over to do the other side. Again, you want to keep the ten degree angle. Stop occasionally mid-stroke and mentally check for the dime's thickness. Repeat the process again and again, slowly eliminating the factory shoulder. The knife is sharp when the planes of the two sides of the blade intersect.

The idea of creating a perfectly sharp edge can be demonstrated by viewing each of the two sharpening angles as a plane. The two planes must cross precisely at the cutting edge to create a burr. As the burr is reduced by honing, a perfectly sharp cutting edge emerges that is straight and reflects no light. A common mistake is to stop sharpening before the two angles cross, resulting in a tiny flat area along the cutting edge.

After some time you will begin to engage the cutting edge on the stone creating a burr. It can be felt with the finger. With continued sharpening you will begin to reduce the burr, until finally it is so thin it breaks away. At that point it is time to switch to the super fine white stone. The white stone hones the sharpened edge, creating a mirror finish on the cutting surface. By polishing the surface, You allow the blade to move smoothly through the wood, reducing the friction and giving you a fluid, easy flow through the wood. Use lighter pressure on the white stone.

A microscopic burr is created during sharpening, and the sharpening is complete when the burr is eliminated. This burr is so small that it is difficult to feel. To find it I hold the blade under direct light and look at the cutting edge from the spine. If there is a burr it will reflect a glint of light in a fine line, and I know I need to sharpen a little more.

Hold the stone in your hand or on a bench and imagine the dime thickness. Rub the blade back and forth on the stone perpendicular to the cutting edge, using medium pressure. When holding the stone in my hand I keep my fingers below the surface of the stone for safety. Focus your attention and pressure on the middle of the cutting edge. If I apply more pressure at the point it puts a slight curve in the cutting edge or rounds the point.

A final check for sharpness involves look straight down on the blade and turning it in the light. If the planes intersect completely, there will be no reflecting of light on the edge of the blade. If they are slightly off, I will see a glint of light.

When to touch up an edge depends on many factors, including the type of wood you are carving. It is not unusual to have to hone a knife soon after it is sharpened. It seems that the more a knife is sharpened the longer it holds its edge. When the knife gets dull, you should be able to get a fresh edge using only the super fine white stone. After many honings you may wish to use the medium stone again to create a new edge.

The bevel of the stab knife is roughly 30 degrees. It is correct as it comes from the factory and the sharpening we do is simply to polish the bevel. Start with the medium stone until you create a fine burr and, then, work it away.

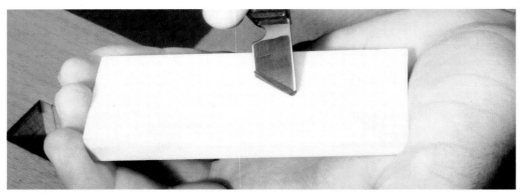

Finish with the white stone.

Hand Positions

The basic blade angle is about 65 degrees, although I vary this at the beginning and end of a cut. The tendency of new carvers is to stand the knife up too much and carving too deeply.

Having used many knives, the ones I've come to prefer are Wayne Barton's, primarily because the length and angle of the blade allows my hand to be close to the work.

The basic motion is to plunge into the wood and follow the line with the cutting edge. At the same time you need to visualize the location of the point of the knife.

There are two hand positions with the carving knife. The primary grip forms a tripod between the knife, the thumb, and the first joint of the forefinger. This gives stability and control to the carving action. I try to keep my thumb and forefinger in contact with the knife handle at all times.

In the second position the first joint of the forefinger rides on the wood, but the knife is rotated so the thumb is putting pressure on the spine. The action is to plunge away from you. The angle of the knife is the same as in the first position. This position is helpful in shapes like triangles and for cleaning up some wood fibers that may have not been cut away.

The stab knife is held as though you were going to stab the work piece.

By pressing it in the wood, it severs the fibers...

and creates an indentation. This can be lengthened and changed by rocking the blade.

Carving Basics

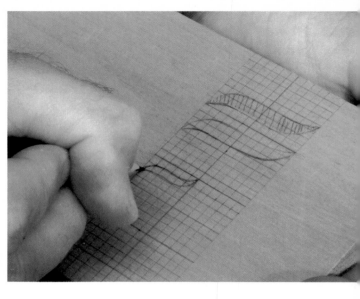

Draw some s-shapes of various sizes using the grid.

A word about safety.

Sharp knives go a long way towards preventing injuries because less pressure is required to manipulate the knife. It is also important to be aware of what you are doing, especially concerning the hand that is holding the work piece. Keep it out of the path of the knife. If you are working on your lap, be especially careful near the edge of the work piece. When working on a small carving on your lap, use a larger piece of wood below the carving to protect your legs.

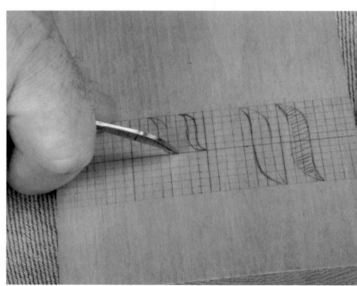

Start with a smaller s-shape. Place the knife in the corner, almost straight up.

To learn the basic strokes I create a grid on a 4" x 12" board of basswood. Basswood is a good wood for beginners. It is easy to carve, available and inexpensive. The grid lines are 1/8" apart.

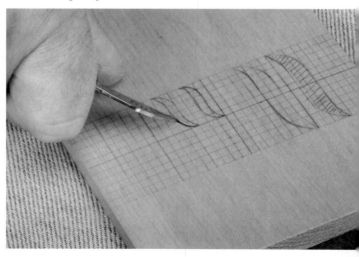

Follow the line, leaning the knife over to about 65 degrees in the middle of the cut.

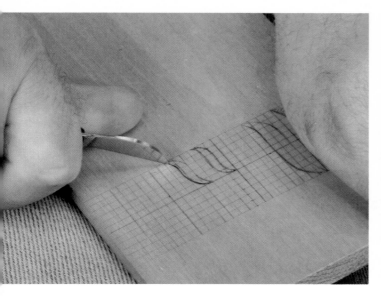

At the end of the cut rotate your wrist so the knife is nearly vertical again.

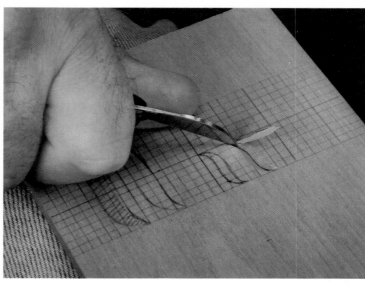

End with the blade vertical. With practice this should free the flowing wedge in the middle...

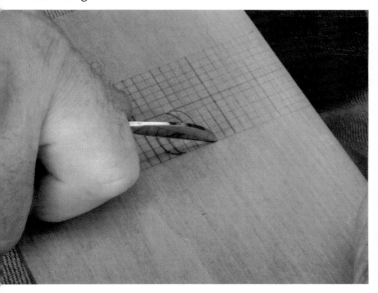

Turn the board around to do the other side. The process is the same. Start at the corner with your knife vertical.

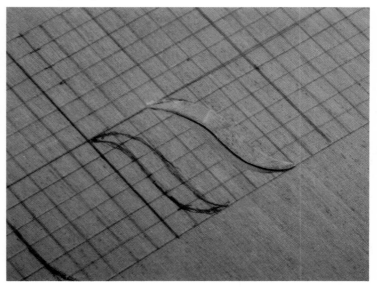

and leave you with this result.

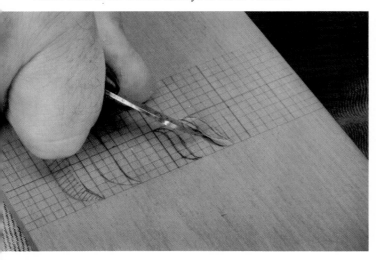

Lean it over as you come down the side.

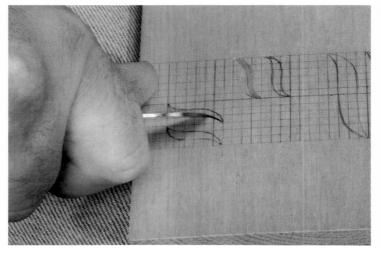

Next draw the mirror image of the s-shape, with the curves going in the opposite direction.

15

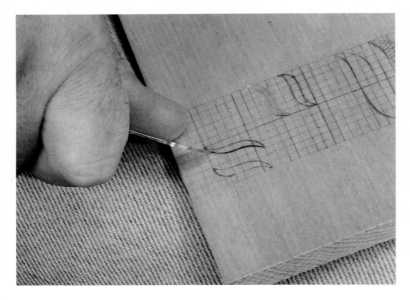

Again start in the corner, but cut the concave curve first. Use a good deal of pressure on this first cut carrying it to the end.

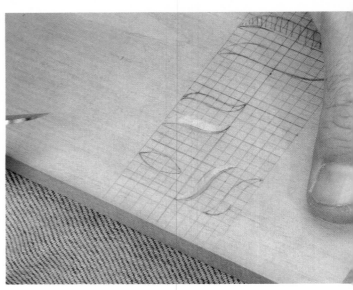

The next practice shape is a pointed oval.

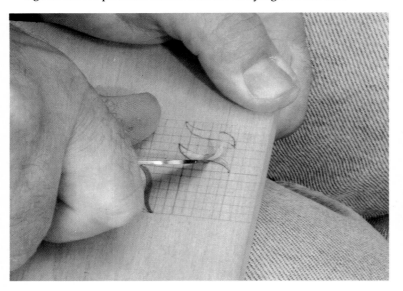

Turn the board and repeat the cut on the other side of the figure. Start in the corner but use only enough pressure to take out the chip, not to undercut the first cut.

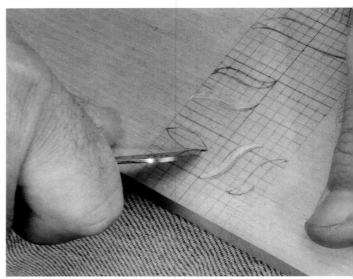

Start at the corner with the knife vertical and shallow.

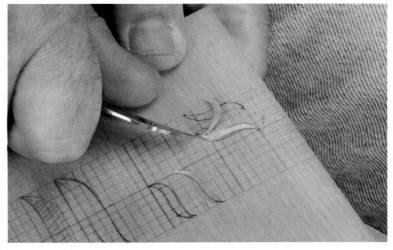

End with the knife blade vertical.

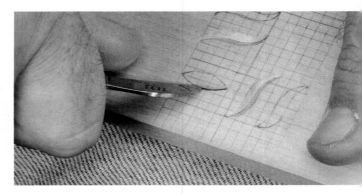

Here you make the transition from cutting with the grain to cutting against the grain. As the blade becomes parallel to the direction of the grain, you must "slip the blade." This is done by sliding the blade slightly out of the cut while continuing your forward progress, severing the wood fibers and preventing the blade from the taking off with the grain.

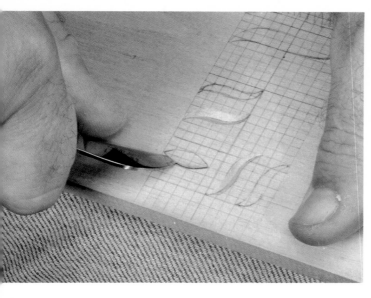

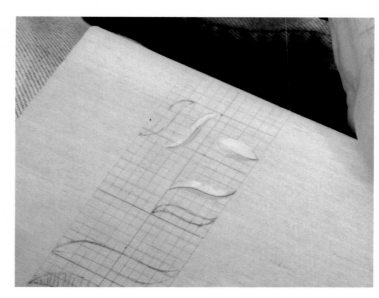

As you continue you can push the knife more deeply into the grain. This may leave some fibers in the trough of the cut, but these are easily cleaned out later if necessary.

The result.

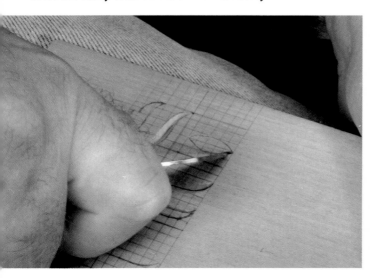

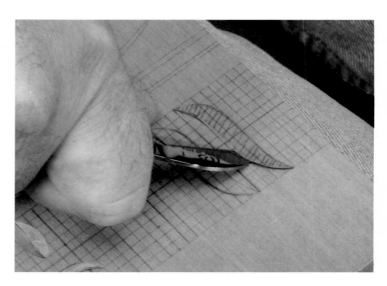

Repeat the process on the other side, starting at the corner...

When you are comfortable with the smaller figures, move to the larger. The technique is the same, but it requires more hand strength. Because you need so much more pressure, be sure the thumb of your holding hand is out of the way in case the knife slips.

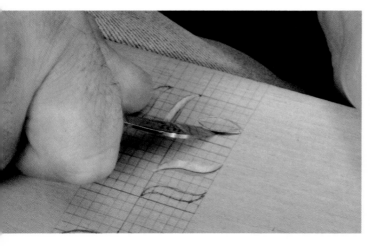

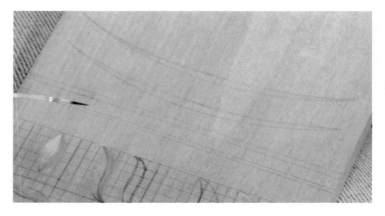

and slipping the blade at the turn. Here the grain is even more likely to tear because it has lost it support.

Next practice straight and curved lines. The two straight lines are of different thicknesses.

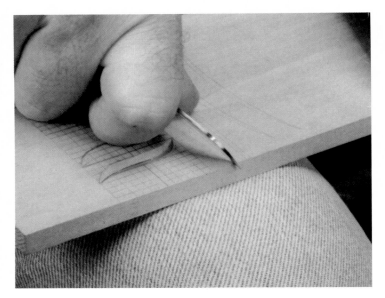

Start at the end. I find it works best if I focus my attention just in front of the blade. When I can do this I always end up with a straighter, more even line.

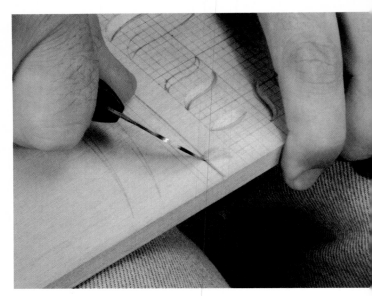

Turn the work and cut the other side of the line. This requires much less pressure, because it is simply a relieving cut. Too much pressure and you undercut the first cut.

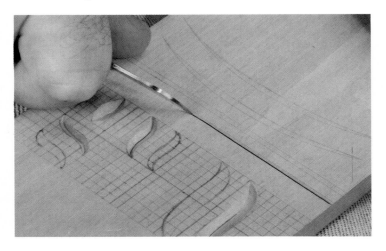

Maintain even pressure through the cut.

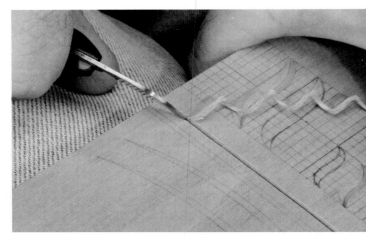

Continue through the line and end it in the same way.

As you approach the end of the cut, your hand leaves the board, making it more difficult to maintain the cutting position. Use your leg or work surface as an extension of the board. At the very end of the cut stop before your knife leaves the board and pivot it down into the wood.

The curved line is cut with the same technique. Focus your attention in front of the blade and keep an even pace and pressure.

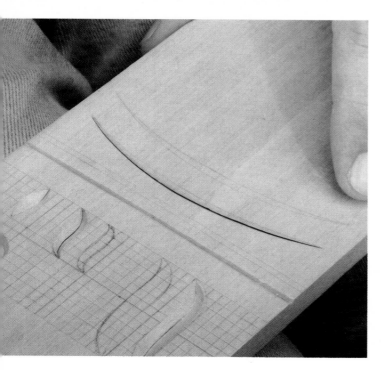

One side of the cut finished. At the ends the blade is more vertical and uses very little pressure.

The concave side is done in the same way, starting shallow and more vertical at the end...

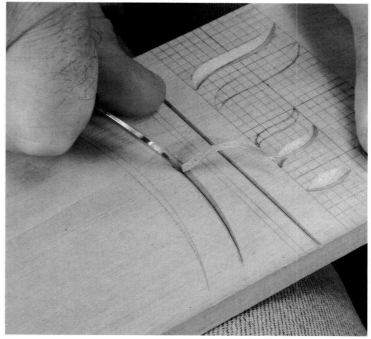

leaning the blade over and going deeper in the middle...

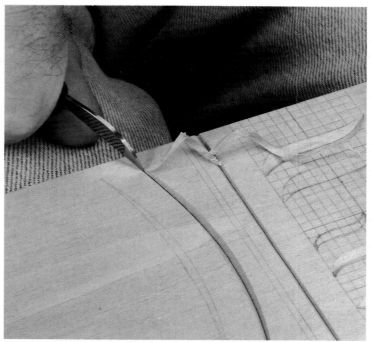

and finishing with the blade vertical and shallow.

Carving
the Bird in the Reeds

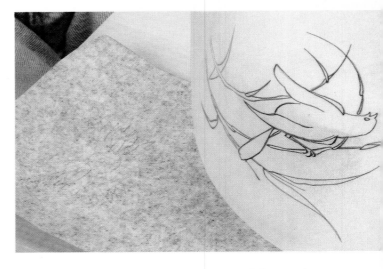

Place graphite paper between the tracing and the wood...
graphite side down!

Trace the pattern onto the board. I use a mechanical pencil
with .5mm lead. A regular pencil gives me a wider line as it
gets dull. Since I don't always cut the line completely away,
this makes more work during the clean-up phase.

For the first project I am using a piece of basswood 3/8"
thick, measuring 9" x 13". It is planed smooth on the work
surface. Other dimensions will work as well, but this fits
nicely on my lap and is easy to use.

Copy the pattern using tracing paper, and tape the tracing to
the wood on one edge.

Ready for carving.

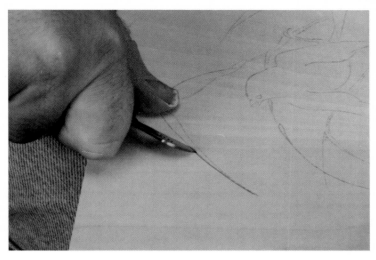

moving deeper in the middle...

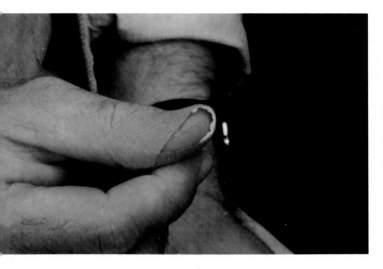

Because finger nails can mar the soft basswood very easily, I wear a band-aid on the thumb of my knife hand. This prevents a lot of scratches and makes clean-up much easier.

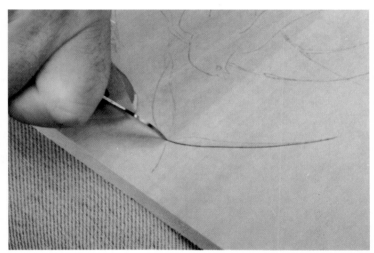

and shallow at the end.

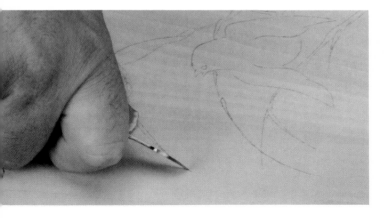

Unlike geometrical chip carving, there is generally no required order here. I usually start at the top or on one side and work my way through the piece. Start at the end of the blade of grass. The pencil line is a guide, but you have some leeway about where your cut actually flows. Start straight up and shallow...

Get shallow as you continue the cut.

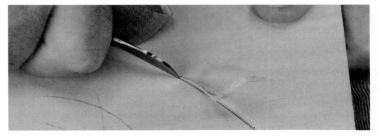

The return cut starts straight up and shallow, but quickly goes deep as the leaf widens at the bottom of this segment.

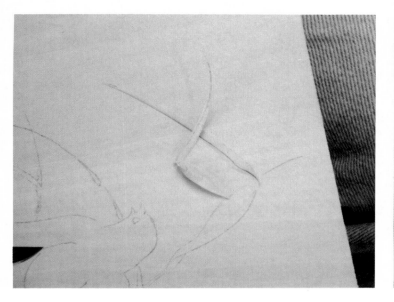

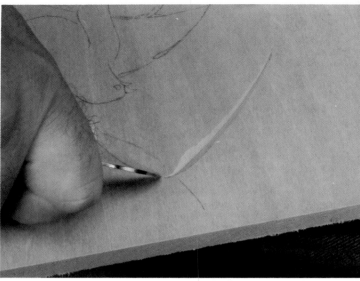

At the deepest point I left some wood in the trough. My goal is to have the chip come out freely and cleanly every time. On wider, deeper cuts, however, this is sometimes difficult.

This middle segment of the leaf begins at the turn at the bottom of the end segment, which I carved first. Start the cut aligned with the previous cut but not touching.

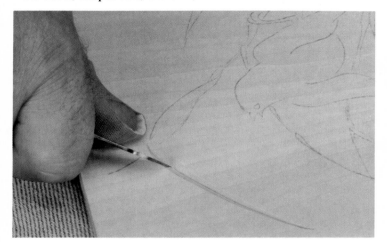

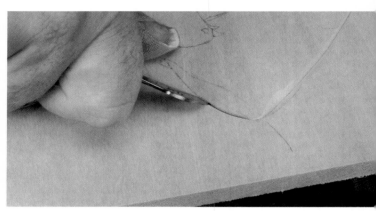

I like to clean it up before continuing, so I lay the side of my blade against the surface of the cut and gently cut into the trough to remove the remaining fibers. Be careful that the point of the blade does not undercut the bottom of the trough.

Lean the knife over as you move to the middle of the cut...

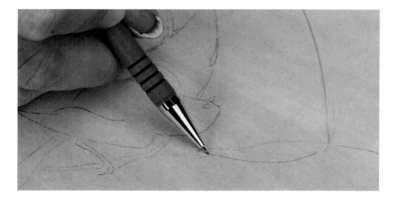

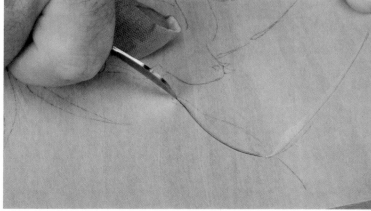

The leaf twists twice, once at the bottom of the first section, and once more here, near its base. Between the small base segment and the longer middle section we need to preserve a ridge. To do this I must make my first cut on the middle section away from the area already carved.

and vertical as you come to the end. Where it crosses the base segment, the point is away from the ridge we want to preserve.

This first cut is considered a stop cut, protecting the ridge while I cut up the other side. On that side, again, I begin shallow and straight...

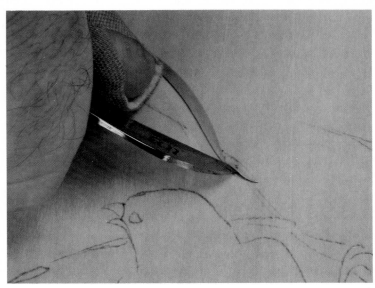

Make the first cut the base portion of the leaf. As a rule you always want to make the first cut so the point of the knife is pointed away from the already carved portion.

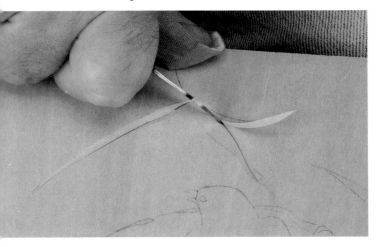

lean it over and go deeper in the middle...

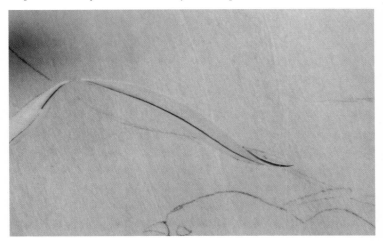

This will leave a strong ridge between these sections, creating the impression of the leaf twisting.

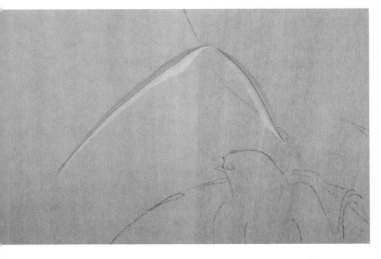

and end up straight and shallow for this result.

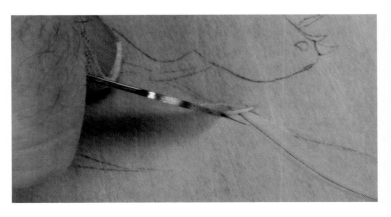

Come back on the other side with a gentle cut using light pressure. You don't want to cut into the wall of the first cut.

The result.

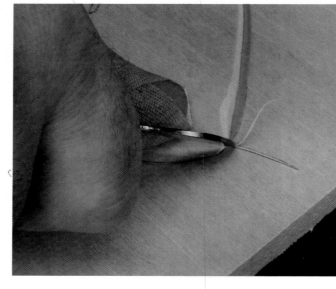

Now start at the tip with very light pressure (almost the weight of the knife is enough) and increase pressure as you move toward the leaf.

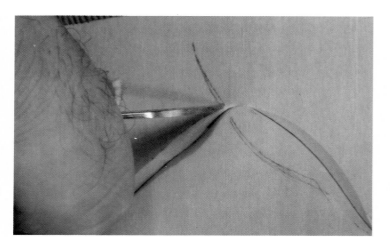

The tip of the stem is a long, thin triangle, requiring a three-sided cut. Following the rule of cutting away from the already cut portion, the first side is a very small stop cut where the stem meets the leaf.

On the other side of the leaf the steam is another long triangle. The first cut is a stop at the leaf, that should match the angle of the cut on the other side.

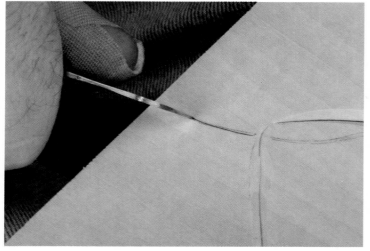

From there cut to the tip of the stem, ending with light pressure.

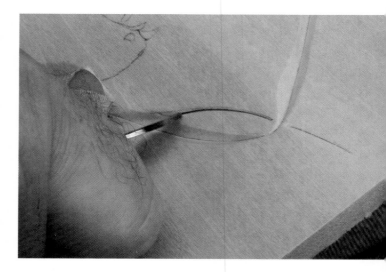

Start from the stop and cut down on side of the stem...

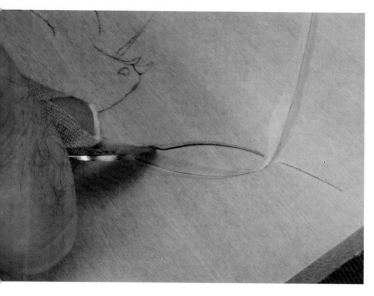

Where the stem meets the leaf again, I give a turn to the cut.

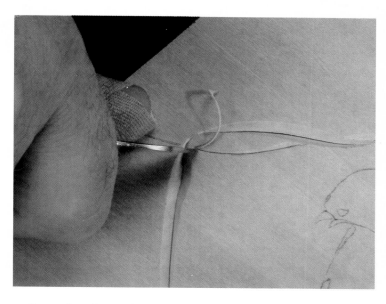

Cut to the other end, trying to match the depth of the cut to the continuation of the stem on the other side of the leaf.

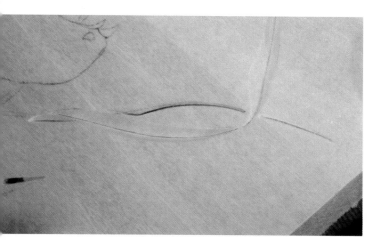

This meets the return line in a little more graceful way than a stop.

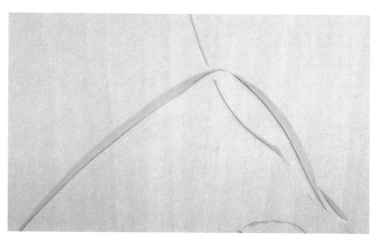

The result. With all chip carving cuts, be careful to start and end a stroke precisely. Any small overcuts will become exaggerated once a finish is applied.

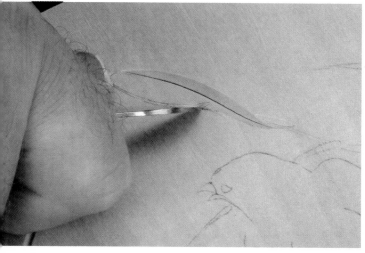

Come up the other side, being careful to begin where the first line ended.

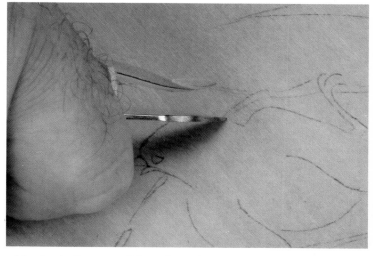

Moving to the next offshoot from the stem, I need a stop at the bird's head.

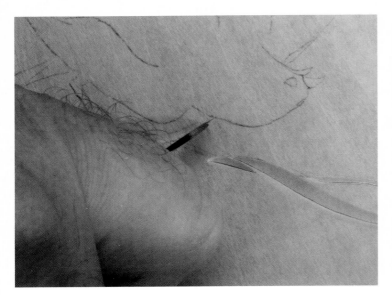

Start at the stop and cut to the rounded end.

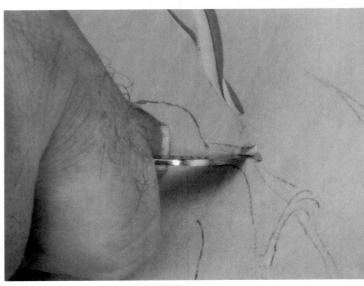

moving back toward the stop cut.

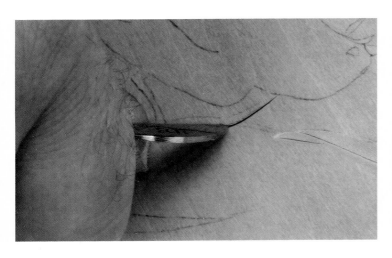

As I approach the end I pivot my blade up so less metal is in the wood. This allows me a tighter turn without affecting my depth.

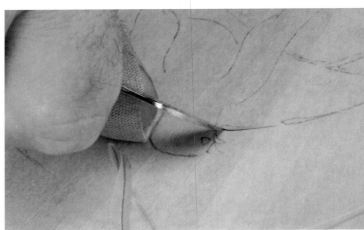

Continue with the grass where it resumes on the other side of the bird. Start at the point, and pivot the blade as you get to the bulbous turn.

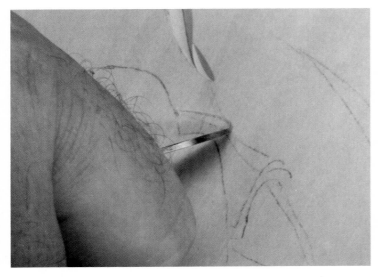

Turn the work and begin cutting where you left off...

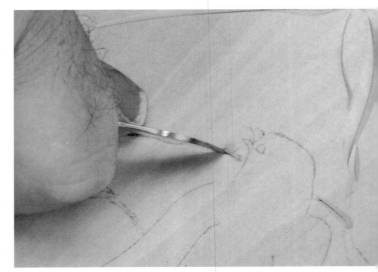

Work from there back to the point.

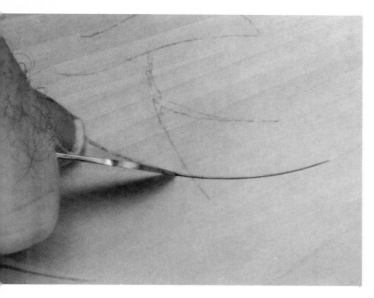

On the longer portion it is important to keep your focus just in front of the blade. Follow the same steps as in the previous segment.

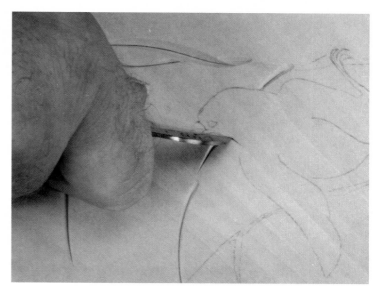

Begin at the lower neck of the bird and cut up to the end of the beak. This makes the cut away from what has already been carved, preventing breakage.

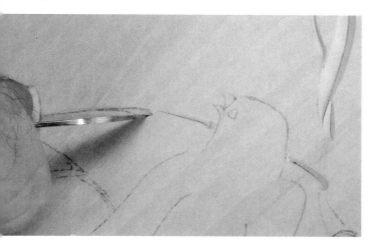

At the bud turn and go back to the point...

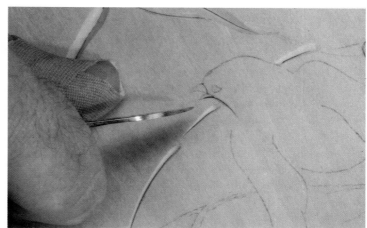

Make a careful turn for a continuous cut.

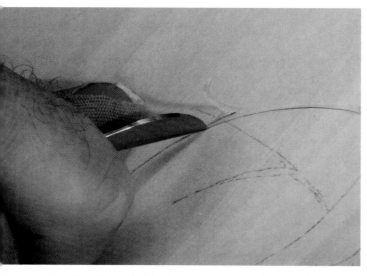

getting skinnier and skinnier as you move closer to the point. Think how graceful the blade of grass is in nature.

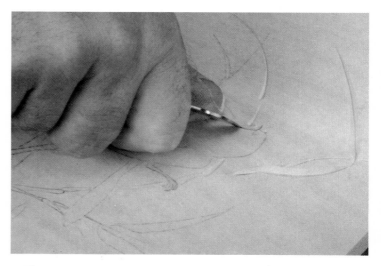

The return cut starts at the tip of the beak, with the knife tip just lightly in the wood. Make a quick turn and come back down the other side of the line.

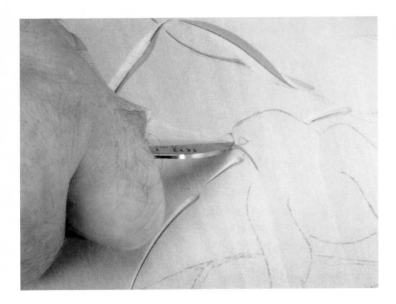

The upper beak is a triangle. It starts with a cut on the lower edge, away from the previous cut.

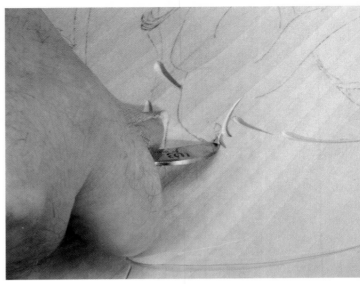

and cut back to the head along the upper curved line.

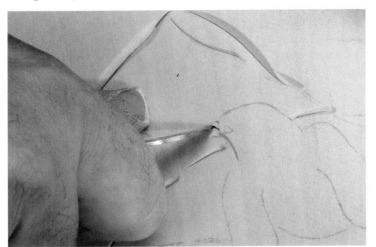

This cut plunges fairly deep and turns at the same time.

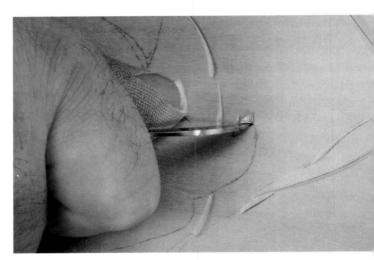

Cut off the triangle at the head with a curving cut.

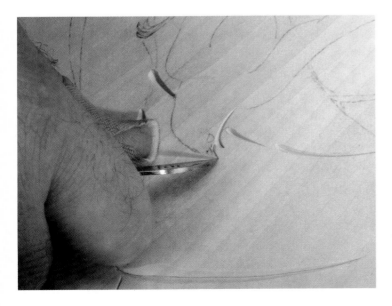

For the second cut, begin at the tip..

The result. The eye will be a curved triangle. Its placement is critical if the bird is to appear realistic, so be sure of your drawing before you begin to carve.

28

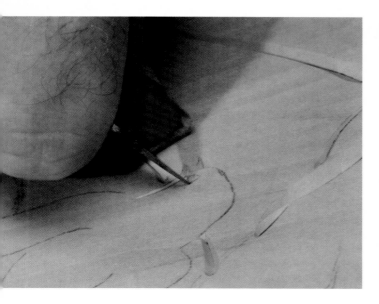

Start at the back corner.

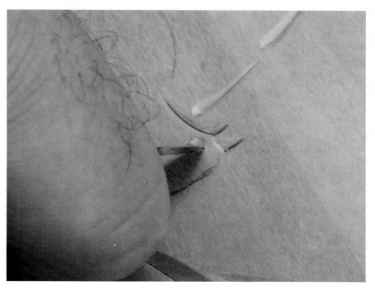

Connect the first two sides of the eye with a third curving cut.

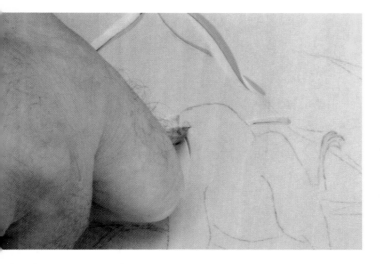

The cut is short, curved, and deep.

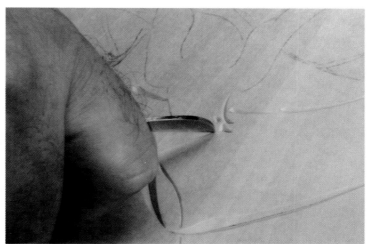

When carving the back of the head, the convex line is cut first. Start at the top of the beak.

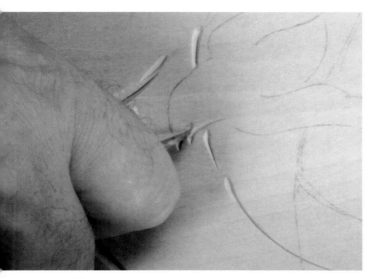

The second cut begins where the first cut ends, and continues up the front edge of the eye. This cut is away from the beak that was already cut, maintaining its strength.

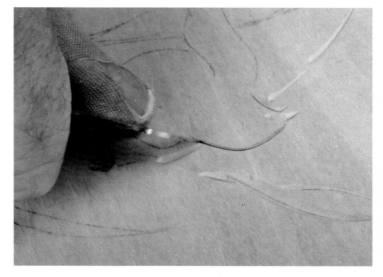

By coming this way you avoid breaking through the previous cut where the leaf meets the head. Instead, you leave a nice clean ridge. Continue to the shoulder.

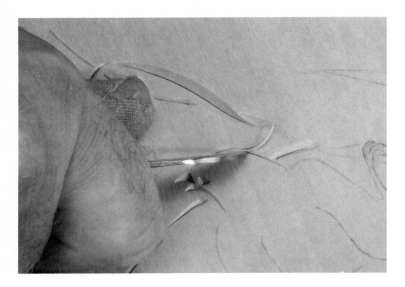

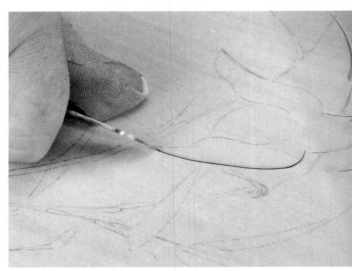

Turn the piece and come back the other way. I almost never use a line that is exactly parallel. Instead I tend to start shallow and finish shallow while going deeper and wider in the middle. This gives the line a sense of life and adds dimension to the carving. The exact location of the deep spot depends on the particular situation. Here on the head, it is at the crown.

Continue a smooth curve down the length of the wing. It gets deeper again at the end.

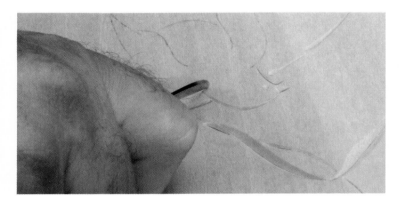

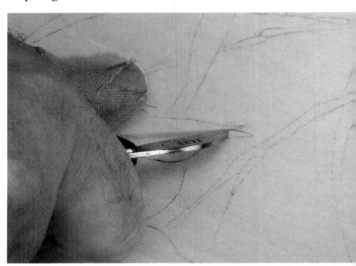

Because the wing is closer to the viewer than the head, I want to start the cut inside the line of the head to give that illusion.

The back cut starts at the tip and goes wide in the beginning portion. This draws the eye to the feather portion of the wing, and gives it more weight.

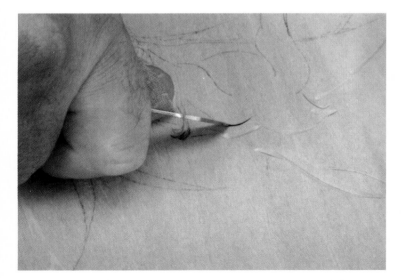

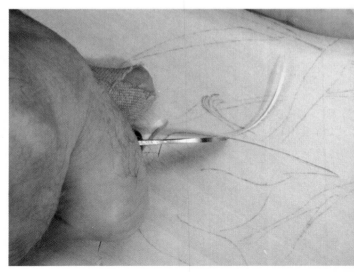

Here I want the deepest part of the cut at the top curve of the wing.

As you move up the wing you get narrower in the middle...

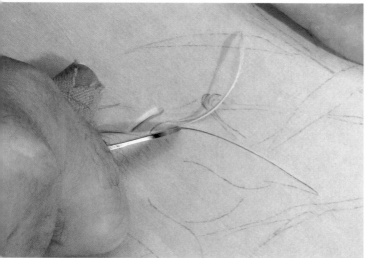

and wider at the top curve.

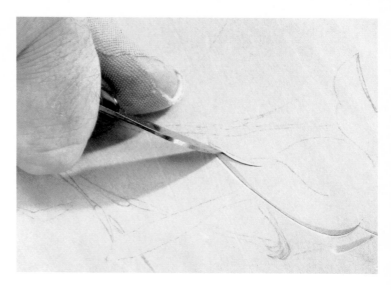

Make a nice crescent cut to the end...

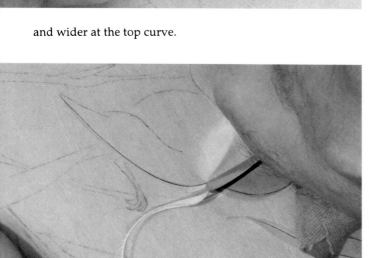

Finally at the end straighten the knife and make the cut shallower.

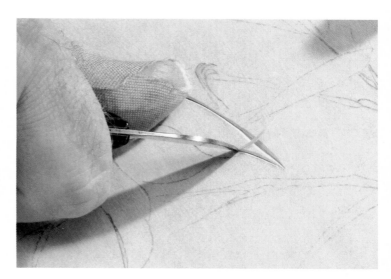

then carve from the end back to the point.

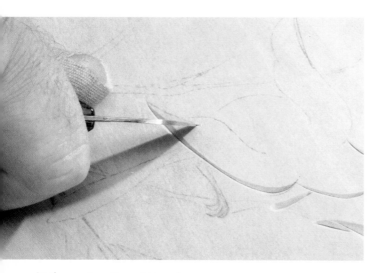

At the next section of the wing, cut toward the tip. This keeps the point of the knife away from what has already been carved.

The same process holds for the next section. Begin at the top...

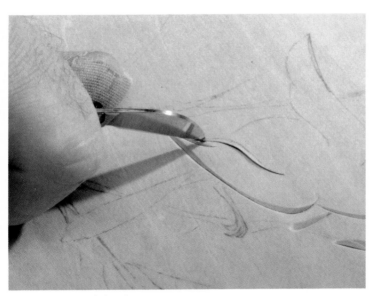

and cut toward the tip.

The return cut starts at the tip.

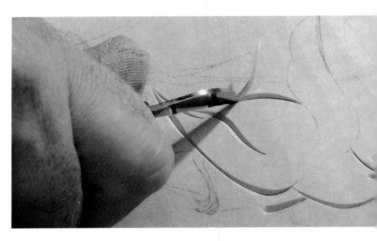

Use a similar crescent cut to carve the back.

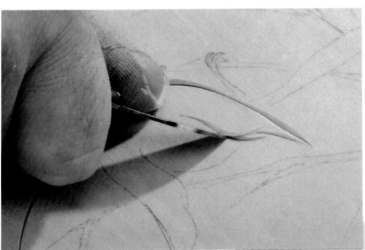

The return cut can be quite bold, creating a sense of shadow.

Progress.

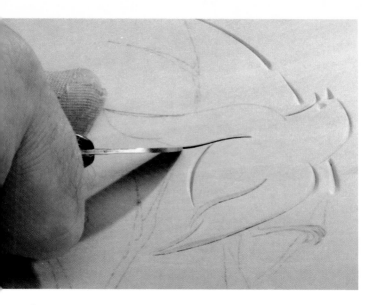

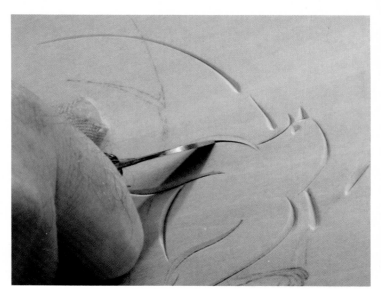

Carve the other wing, working away from the previous cuts. If the curve causes you to cross over the grain, slip the blade so the tip is slicing and not drawn into the direction of the grain.

No matter which way you go on this last wing cut you will be cutting toward a previous carving. I choose to start at the head because the throat cut is with the grain and is less likely to break.

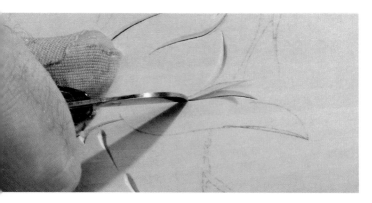

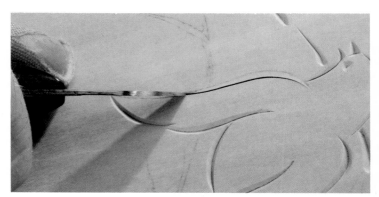

Return cut in the opposite direction.

I've decided to break this long line into two segments, stopping here with the first segment.

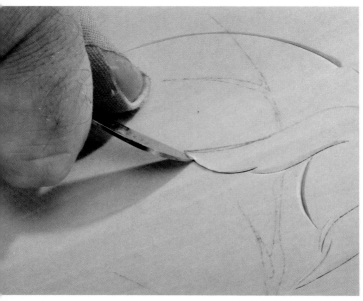

The end segment goes across the grain so will need some extra knife pressure.

The return cut can go pretty deep at the curve of the wing.

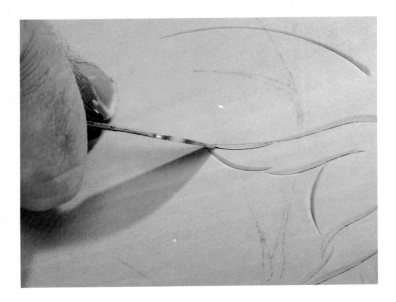

For the second segment, start a little within the previous line and cut down to the tip.

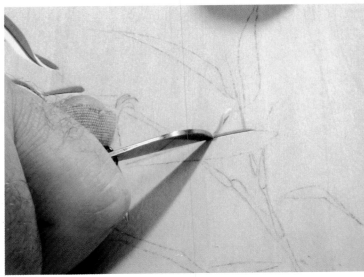

Keep the return thin. You want the other edge of the tail, at the bottom, to be in shadow, and so carved wider, adding visual weight.

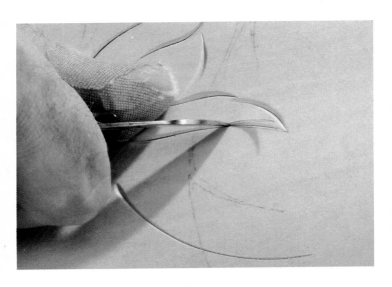

Make the return to complete the wings.

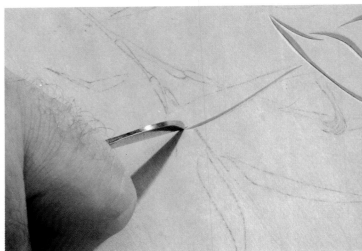

To create the suggestion of feathers, start inside the end of the first tail line...

Carve the tail away from the body, stopping before the end.

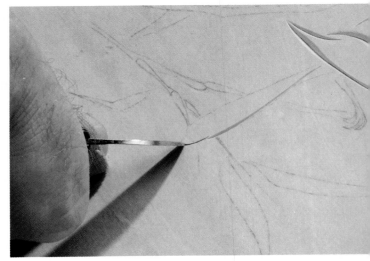

and cut to the tip of the tail make the return cut.

34

HOCK TOOLS - Price List 2013

Bench Plane Blades	BP010	O1: Blade for #10 & 10½-type Rabbet Planes	$49.00
	BP040	O1: Blade for #40-type Scrub Planes	$39.00
	BP175	O1: 1¾" Blade for Stanley/Record-type #3 Bench Planes	$38.00
	BP200	O1: 2" Blade for Stanley/Record-type #4 & #5 Bench Planes	$40.00
	BP225	O1: 2¼" Blade for Stanley #5½ Bench Planes	$42.00
	BP238	O1: 2-3/8" Blade for Stanley/Record-type #4½, 5½, 6 & 7 Planes	$42.00
	BP262	O1: 2-5/8" Blade for Stanley/Record-type #8 Bench Planes	$46.00
	BPA175	A2 Cryo: 1¾" Blade for Stanley/Record-type #3 Bench Planes	$50.00
	BPA200	A2 Cryo: 2" Blade for Stanley/Record #4 & 5 Bench Planes	$51.00
	BPA225	A2 Cryo: 2¼" Blade for Stanley-type #5½ Bench Planes	$52.00
	BPA238	A2 Cryo: 2-3/8" Blade for Stanley/Record #4½, 5½, 6 & 7 Planes	$52.00
	BPA262	A2 Cryo: 2-5/8" Blade for Stanley/Record-type #8 Bench Planes	$53.00
Cap Irons	BK175	1¾" Cap Iron for Stanley/Record-type #3 Bench Planes	$28.00
	BK200	2" Cap Iron for Stanley/Record-type #4 & #5 Bench Planes	$30.00
	BK225	2¼" Cap Iron for Stanley #5½ Bench Planes	$32.00
	BK238	2-3/8" Cap Iron for Stanley/Record-type #4½, 5½, 6 & 7 Planes	$32.00
	BK262	2-5/8" Cap Iron for Stanley/Record-type #8 Bench Planes	$38.00
Blade & Cap Iron Sets	BBS175	O1: 1¾" Blade & Cap Iron for Stanley/Record-type #3	$65.00
	BBS200	O1: 2" Blade & Cap Iron for Stanley/Record-type #4 & #5	$69.00
	BBS225	O1: 2¼" Blade & Cap Iron for Stanley #5½ Planes	$73.00
	BBS238	O1: 2-3/8" Blade & Cap Iron for Stanley-type #4½, 5½, 6 & 7	$73.00
	BBS262	O1: 2-5/8" Blade & Cap Iron for Stanley-type #8 Planes	$81.00
	BAS175	A2 Cryo: 1¾" Blade & Cap Iron for Stanley-type #3 Bench Planes	$77.00
	BAS200	A2 Cryo: 2" Blade & Cap Iron for Stanley/Record-type #4 & #5	$80.00
	BAS225	A2 Cryo: 2¼" Blade & Cap Iron for Stanley #5½ Planes	$82.00
	BAS238	A2 Cryo: 2-3/8" Blade & Cap Iron for Stanley-type #4½, 5½, 6 & 7	$83.00
	BAS262	A2 Cryo: 2-5/8" Blade & Cap Iron for Stanley-type #8 Planes	$91.00
Block Plane Blades	BL138	O1: 1-3/8"" Block Plane Blade with 7/16"" wide slot	$34.00
	BL162	O1: 1-5/8"" Block Plane Blade with 7/16"" wide slot	$37.00
	BLA138	A2 Cryo: 1-3/8" Block Plane Blade with 7/16"" wide slot	$48.00
	BLA162	A2 Cryo: 1-5/8"" Block Plane Blade with 7/16"" wide slot	$50.00
	BW138	O1: 1-3/8"" Block Plane Blade with 5/8" wide slot	$34.00
	BW162	O1: 1-5/8"" Block Plane Blade with 5/8" wide slot	$37.00
	BWA138	A2 Cryo: 1-3/8" Block Plane Blade with 5/8" wide slot	$48.00
	BWA162	A2 Cryo: 1-5/8" Block Plane Blade with 5/8" wide slot	$50.00
Kits	KB100	Mini Krenov-style Block Plane Kit, Bubinga with 1" wide Blade	$63.00
	KF150	Krenov-style Plane Kit, Jarrah with 1½" Plane Iron	$105.00
	KS075	Shoulder Plane Kit, Bubinga and Beech with ¾" Wide Blade	$95.00
	KSP062	Wooden Spokeshave Kit, Jarrah with 4-7/16" blade	$84.00
Marking Knives	MK025	O1: ¼" x 7" Marking Knife Blade, "Spear" Point	$30.00
	MK075	O1: ¾" x 7" Marking Knife Blade, "Spear" Point	$33.00
Kitchen Knife Kits	KP350	O1: 3½" Paring Knife Kit	$35.00
	KC500	O1: 5" Chef's Knife Kit	$50.00
	KC800	O1:8" Chef's Knife Kit	$70.00
	KS800	O1: 8" Slicing/Carving Knife Kit	$50.00

Carving Knives	CK100	O1: 1" Carving Knife with Bubinga Handle	$32.00
	CK125	O1: 1¼" Carving Knife with Bubinga Handle	$32.00
	CKC100	O1: 1" Chip Carving Knife with Bubinga Handle	$32.00
	CKS125	O1: 1¼" Chip Carving Stab Knife with Bubinga Handle	$32.00
	CKX125	O1: 1¼" Detail Knife with Bubinga Handle	$32.00
Krenov-style Blades	PI100	O1: 1" x 3½" Krenov-Style Blade & Cap Iron	$42.00
	PI125	O1: 1¼" x 3½" Krenov-Style Blade & Cap Iron	$45.00
	PI150	O1: 1½" x 3½" Krenov-Style Blade & Cap Iron	$48.00
	PI175	O1: 1¾" x 3½" Krenov-Style Blade & Cap Iron	$52.00
	PI200	O1: 2" x 3½ Krenov-Style Blade & Cap Iron	$55.00
	PL100	O1: 1" x 4½" Krenov-Style Blade & Cap Iron	$47.00
	PL125	O1: 1¼" x 4½" Krenov-Style Blade & Cap Iron	$49.00
	PL150	O1: 1½"x 4½" Krenov-Style Blade & Cap Iron	$52.00
	PL175	O1: 1¾" x 4½" Krenov-Style Blade & Cap Iron	$57.00
	PL200	O1: 2" x 4½" Krenov-Style Blade & Cap Iron	$59.00
	PR125	O1: 1¼" x 3½" x 4"radius-edge Blade & Cap Iron	$49.00
	PR150	O1: 1½" x 3½" x 5"radius-edge Blade & Cap Iron	$53.00
	PR175	O1: 1¾" x 3½" x 6"radius-edge Blade & Cap Iron	$55.00
Scraper Blades	SB080	O1: Blade for #80-style Scraper Plane	$28.00
	SB081	O1: Blade for #81-style Scraper Plane	$28.00
	SB112	O1: Blade for #112-style Scraper Plane	$34.00
Knife Blades	VK025	O1: ¼" x 7" Violin Knife Blade - Double Bevel	$31.00
	VK025L	O1: ¼" x 7" Violin Knife Blade – Left Hand Bevel	$31.00
	VK025R	O1: ¼" x 7" Violin Knife Blade – Right Hand Bevel	$31.00
	VK050	O1: ½" Violin Knife Blade – Double Bevel	$32.00
	VK050L	O1: ½" Violin Knife Blade – Left Hand Bevel	$32.00
	VK050R	O1: ½" Violin Knife Blade – Right Hand Bevel	$32.00
	VK075	O1: ¾" Violin Knife Blade – Double Bevel	$33.00
	VK075L	O1: ¾" Violin Knife Blade – Left Hand Bevel	$33.00
	VK075R	O1: ¾" Violin Knife Blade – Right Hand Bevel	$33.00
Spokeshave Blades	SP044	O1: Small (2½") Wooden Spokeshave Blade	$39.00
	SP062	O1 Large (4-7/16") Wooden Spokeshave Blade	$40.00
	SP151	O1: Blade for #151 Spokeshave	$33.00
	SP175	O1: 1¾" Spokeshave Blade with "U" slot	$29.00
	SP200	O1: 2" Spokeshave Blade with "U" slot, 3/32" thick	$30.00
	SP200X	O1: 2" Spokeshave Blade with "U" slot, 5/64" thick	$30.00
	SPA151	A2 Cryo: Blade for #151 Spokeshave	$42.00
Misc	SH075	O1: ¾" x 5" Tee Shoulder Plane Blade	$30.00
	BR375	O1: 3/8 x 6" Burnishing Rod Rc64+	$16.00
	SC075	Scratch Stock	$32.00
	SC075-4	Scratch Stock Blades 4-pack	$6.50
	AP100	HOCK Apron	$20.00

www.HOCKTOOLS.com

HOCK TOOLS 711 B North Main Street, Fort Bragg, California 95437 888-282-5233 ron@hocktools.com

4-15

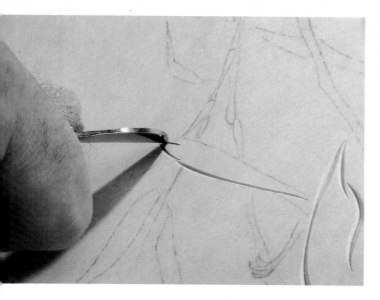

Cut the other side of the end of the tail, carving toward the tip, away from the previous cut...

and back.

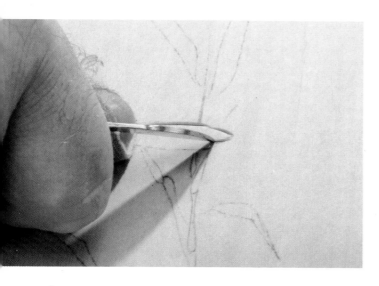

and returning.

With the added thickness, this line is obviously the bottom.

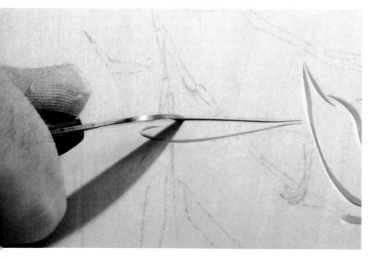

The final line of the tail should be thicker. Work away from the chip by carving toward the tip...

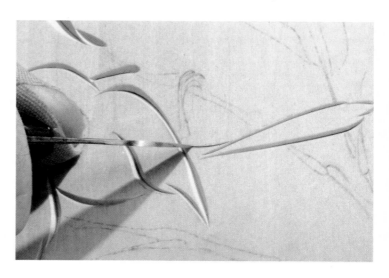

The line of the base of the tail is a simple curve.

This gives a sense of thickness to the tail.

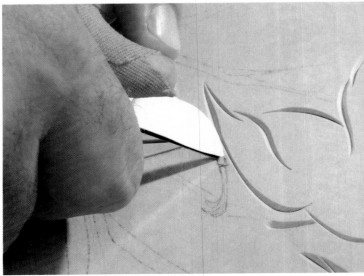

For the third cut a hand position change is necessary. Place your thumb on the top of the blade so you can push the blade away from you rather than pull it toward you. Start at the top and follow the outer line. This cuts with the grain for a smooth cut.

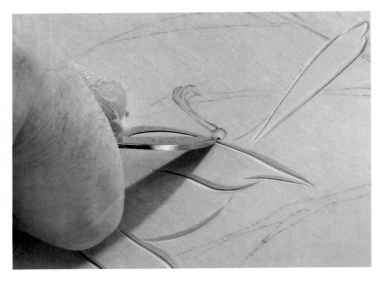

Make a plunge cut where the upper leg meets the body. This preserves the ridge between them.

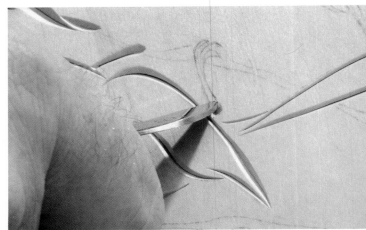

Make a stop at the top of the lower leg, leaving a ridge where it meets the upper leg.

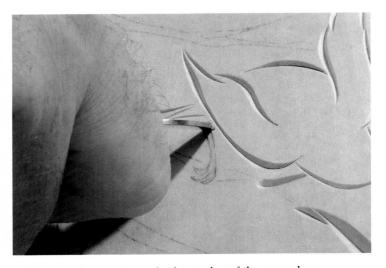

The second cut is along the front edge of the upper leg.

From the ridge cut down the front of the leg with a fairly shallow cut.

The line continues to the toes, but you don't want the toes to be perfectly round. Some suggestion of the jointed segments should remain.

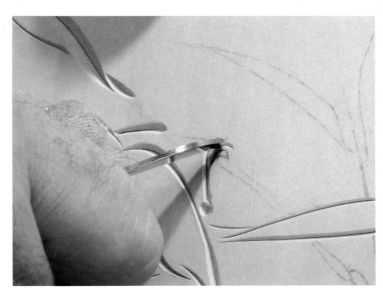

Make the return to relieve the first cut, also in segmented cuts.

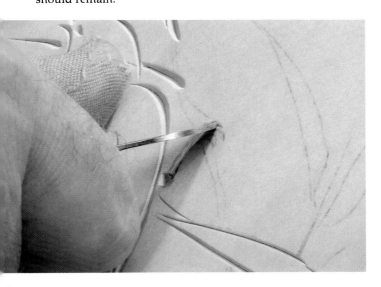

Cut from the end of the toe back up to the stop.

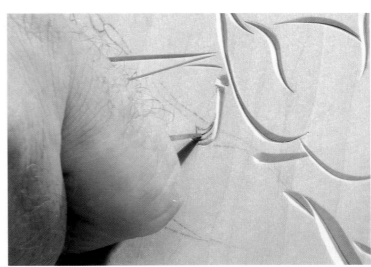

Do the third toe in the same way. It is helpful to choke up on the knife to gain accuracy.

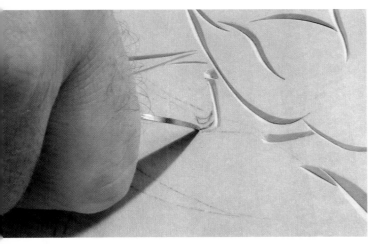

Cut the middle toe in the same way, leaving bumps to suggest the joints.

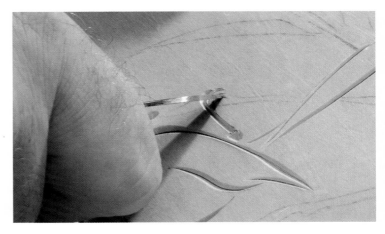

With the grain running in this direction we can use three distinct cuts for the return, emphasizing the jointed nature of the claw. Cut one..

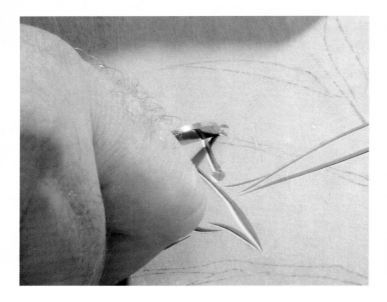

Cut two...

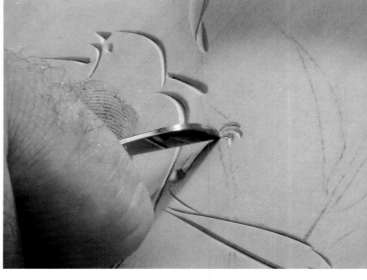

Cut three.

The completed bird.

With the feet complete we can carve the branch on which he hangs.

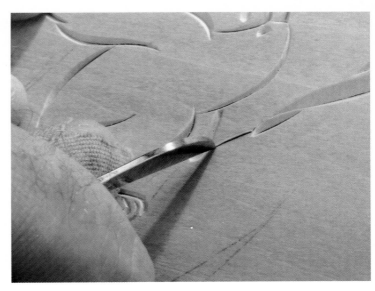

Even with the stop, there is only a thin wall to keep your knife from straying. Cut with care here.

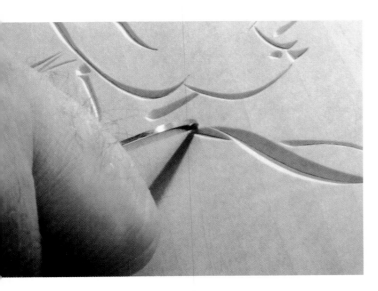

When working around already carved portions it is important to create stops. I put a stop...

Turn the board and make the return cut.

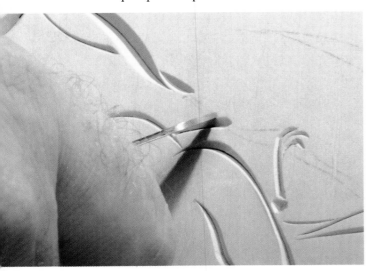

at each end of the segment.

Follow the same steps on the next segment.

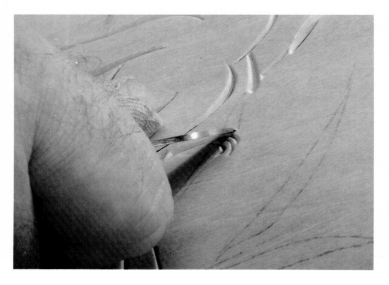

Above the toe I want more of a space than a ridge, so I move away from the foot to make my stop.

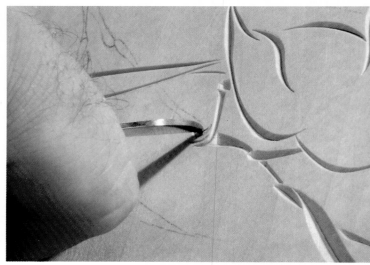

Beneath the foot I keep the stop as close as possible. I think it helps him look like he is hanging on. It is a curved stop.

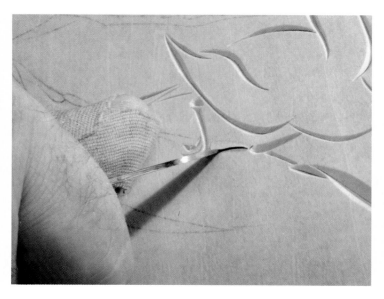

This is a fairly wide cut so you need to push the knife in further.

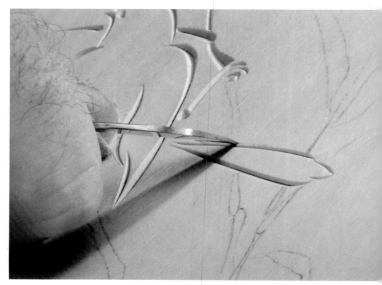

Cut a stop above the tail...

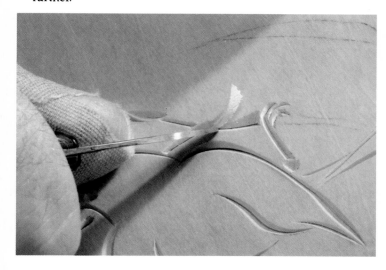

Complete the cut, starting deep and easing up.

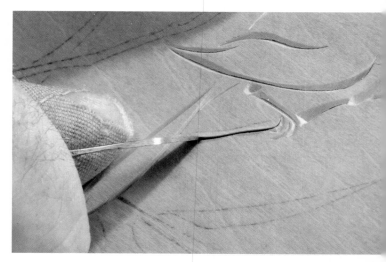

and cut from the foot to the tail.

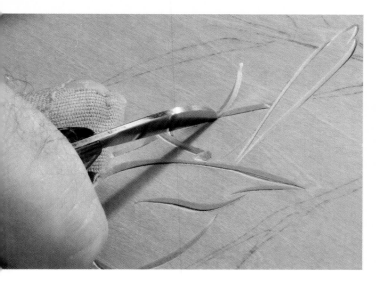

On the return cut remember to vary the thickness of the line.

Cut from there to the point of the segment...

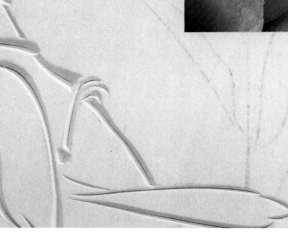

Progress.

and from the point back to the tail.

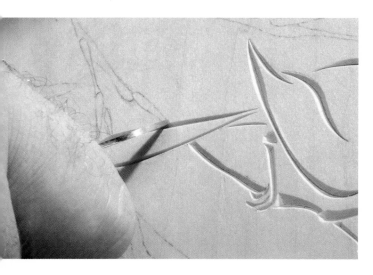

Cut a stop in the stem below the tail.

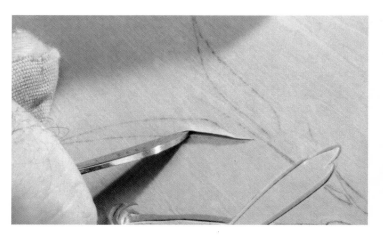

Because the next segment of the stem I was working on intersects with the stem to its right, I want to cut the right stem first. Start with the leaf, running the blade deep and flat to cover the width.

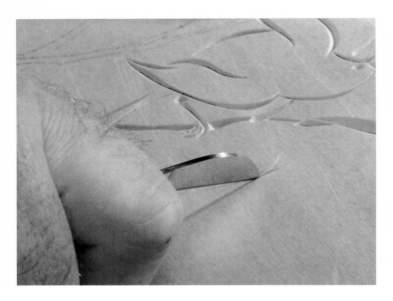

Cut the return starting at the tip of the leaf with the blade shallow and upright.

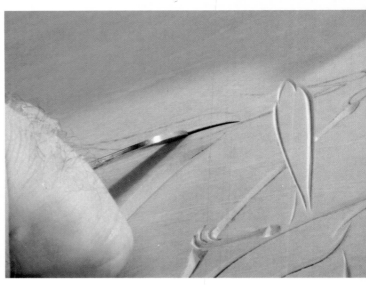

The other leaf on this stem is challenging because it flows with the grain. Begin at the base with the blade straight up.

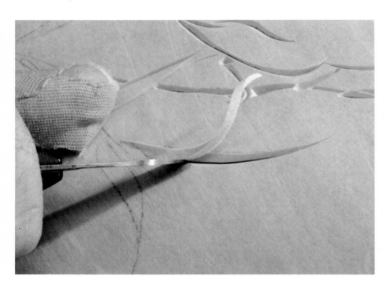

Lean it over toward the middle...

Lay the blade over and go deep along the edge.

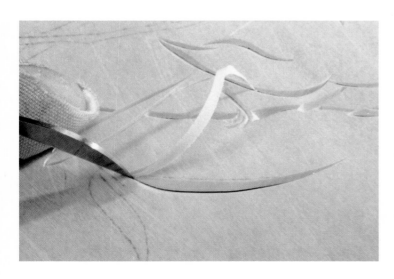

and end with it upright and shallow.

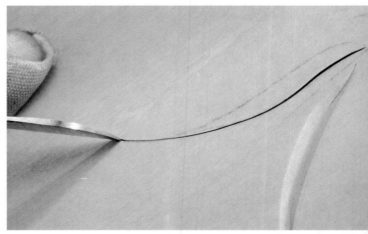

As you reach the turn, slip the blade to cut the fibers without being drawn into the grain. End with the blade vertical and shallow.

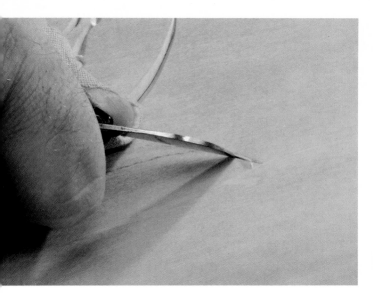

The return cut is similar. Start shallow and straight.

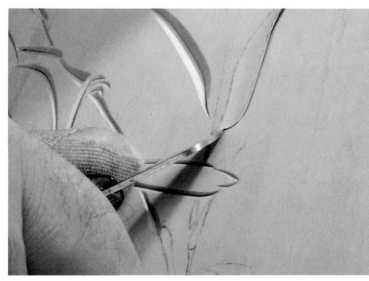

End with the blade upright and shallow.

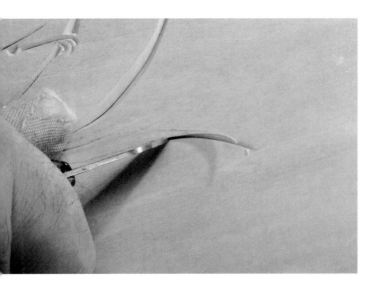

At the turn slip the blade.

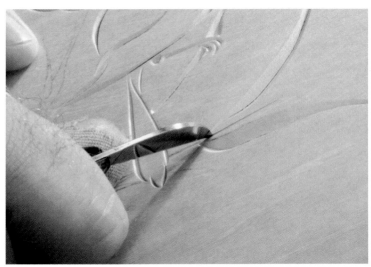

Cut the delicate stem between the leaves.

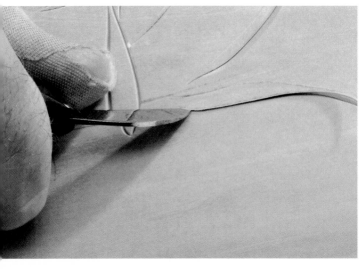

Lay the blade and go deep.

To avoid parallel lines, give the stem a little swell above the bird's tail.

43

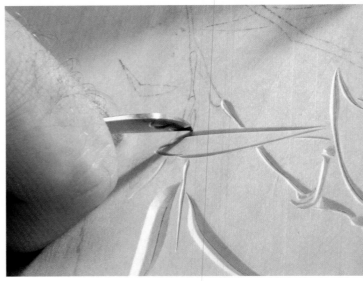

While we are up here we can carve the point of another stem. It is a simple arc cut, up...

Below the tail continue the stems of grass. This one requires the slightest stop cut. Use the tip of the knife.

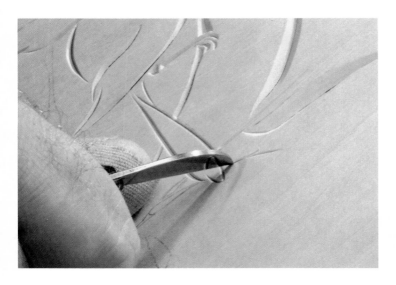

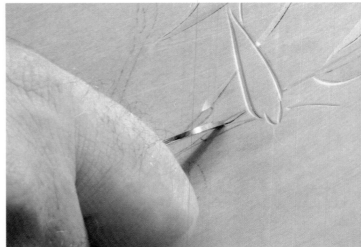

and back.

Progress.

Cut down to the base widening the cut.

The return cut should start wide and taper back to the stop.

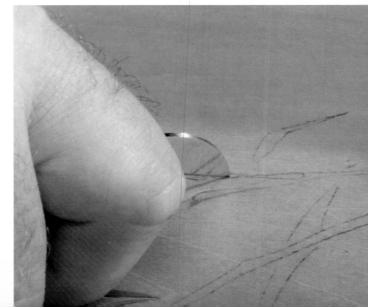

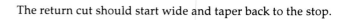

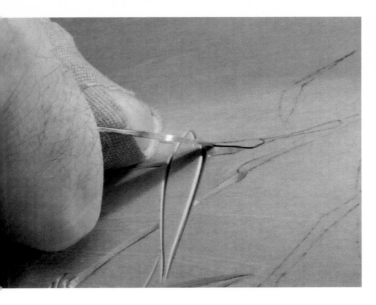

Cut away from the first stem working up the second.

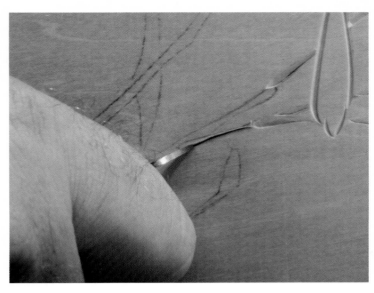

Come down from the stop to create a bulbous base.

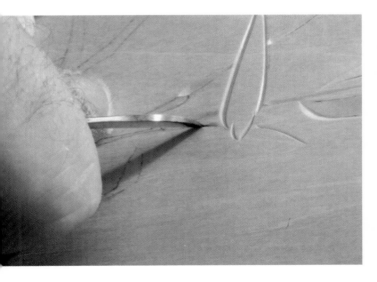

Come up to a point below the tail and return on the other side.

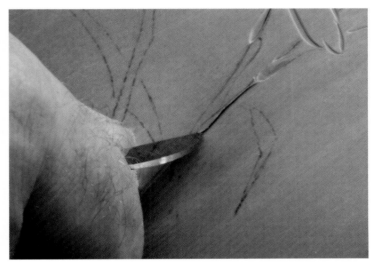

Lift your knife slightly to make the turn...

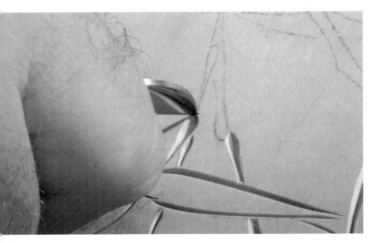

A short concave stop is at the end of the next segment.

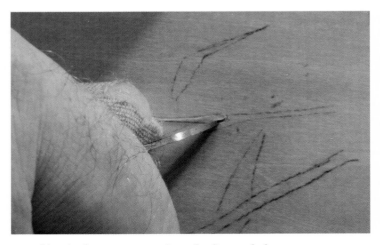

and begin the return cut where the first ended.

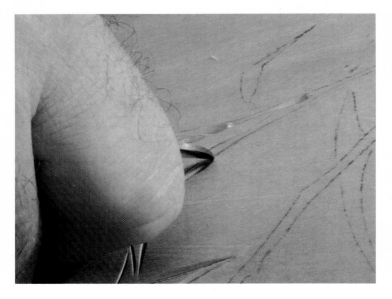

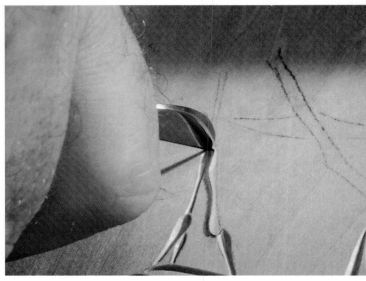

The next segment is rather complex. It begins with a short stop cut at the top.

Cut across the stem and continue the cut...

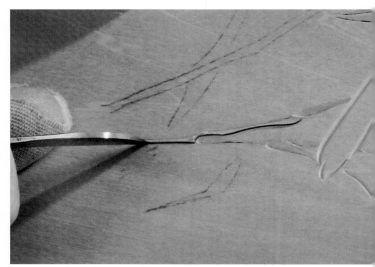

From there it is a continuous cut to the intersection with the adjoining stem.

to follow the stem to the end.

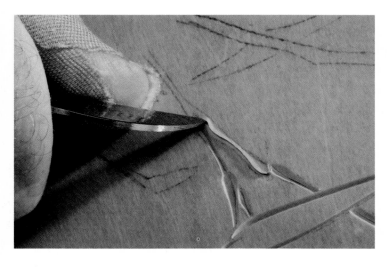

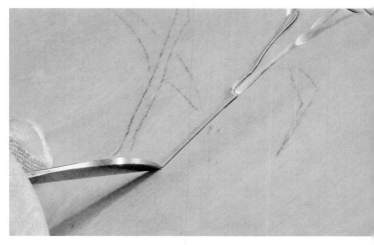

Slip the knife to get around here.

Cut across the end with a stop...

Then return up the other side.

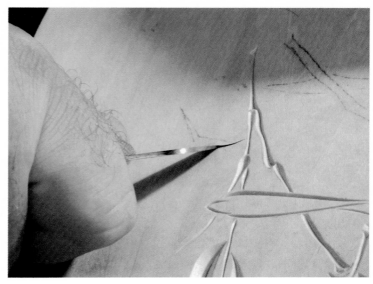

The small leaf starts shallow at the stem gets deep at the turn...

Go deeper at the wide points.

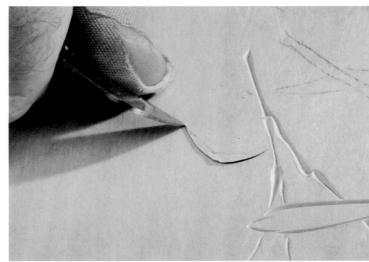

and returns to shallow at the end.

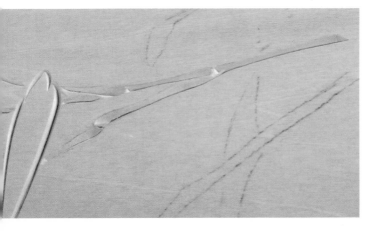

With a complicated cut like this we expect to have some rough spots. In fact there are only two here, and they are easy to clean up.

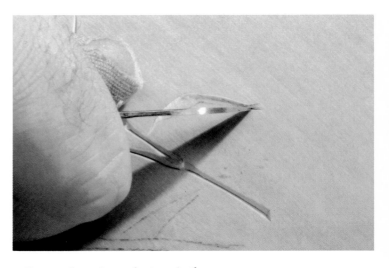

Start at the point and return in the same way.

47

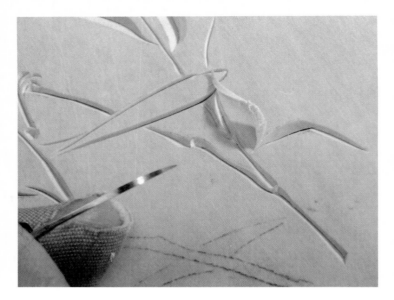

The result.

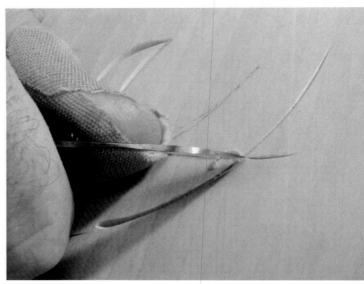

Return from the point, again jumping over the leaf...

Moving to the other stem I start at the end. Cut a stop at the first leaf.

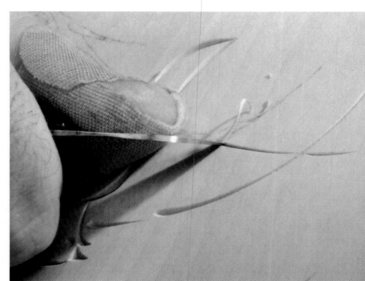

and ending the rather straight cut with a deeper, wider base.

From there cut to the end of the stem lifting blade out of the wood to go over the previously cut leaf and continuing on the other side to the end.

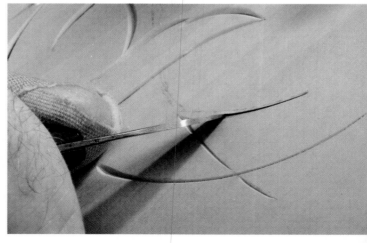

The leaf is a two-sided cut...

widening at the base.

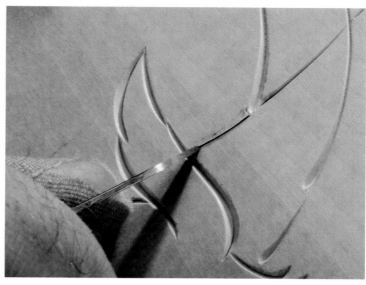

Cut the line. It helps sever the fibers at the stop cut if you lift the handle a little bit, forcing the point down into the corner.

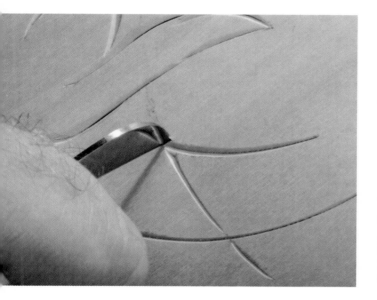

Continue with the stem below the leaf, making a curved stop cut there....

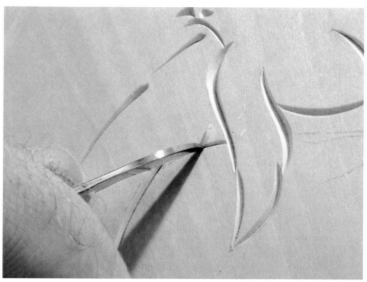

Return on the other side.

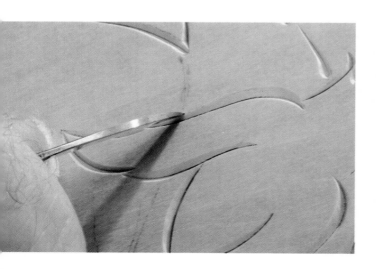

and one at the wing.

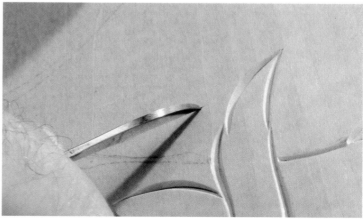

Before cutting the lower stem, I need to cut the small shoot. It is a two cut line starting at the tip and going to the stem.

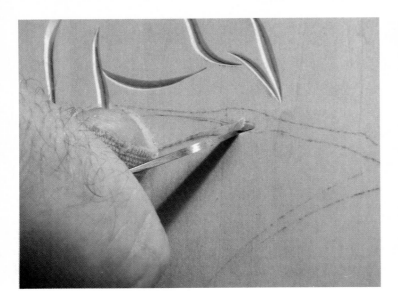

The return starts at the stem with a fairly deep plunge and tapers out to the tip.

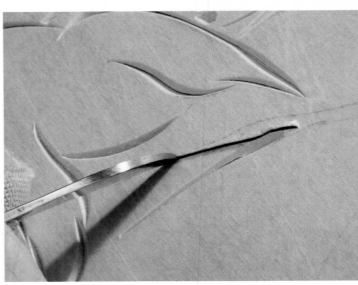

From the stop cut at the shoot, cut back to the wing. This works away from the carving of the shoot.

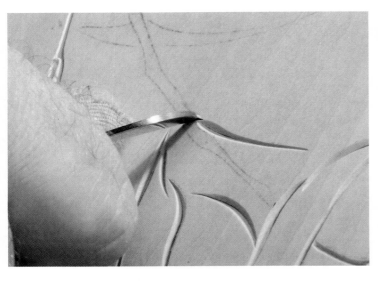

For protection cut a stop at the base of the shoot, carrying it into the middle of the stem. It will be cut away later.

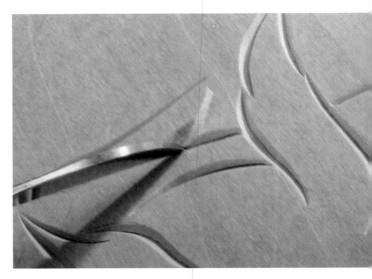

Cut from the wing to the end of the stem.

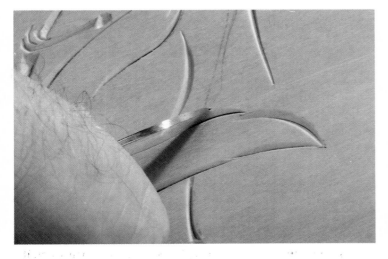

Make a stop on the stem below the wing.

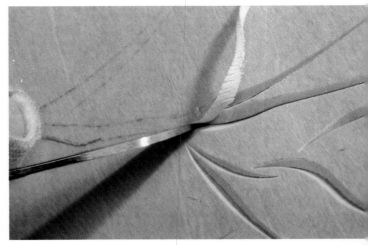

At the shoot cut more deeply...

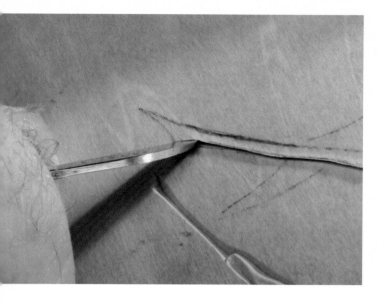

and at the end of the cut, raise your knife up to sever the fiber.

Cut back to the shoot.

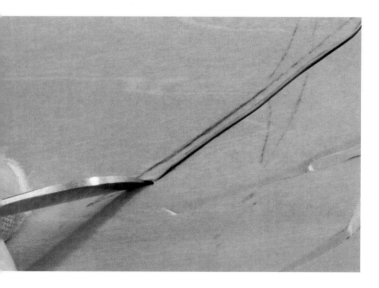

The bottom cut starts with a plunge...

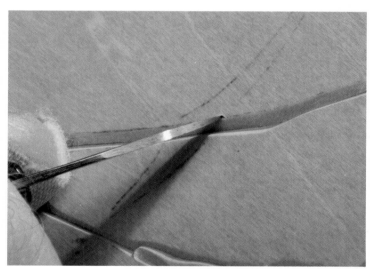

Finally we have a leaf that goes behind the stem. Cut a stop at the stem.

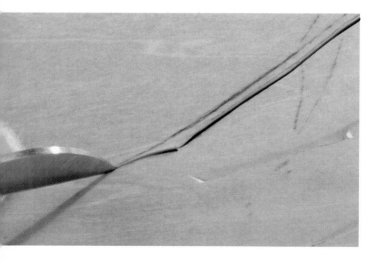

and tapers up at the point.

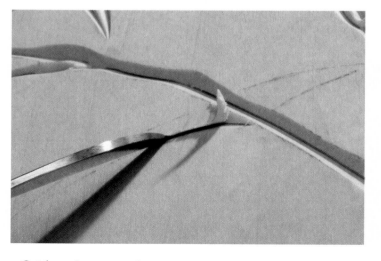

Cut from the stem to the tip...

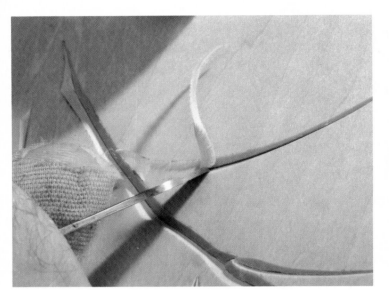

and back from the tip to the stem.

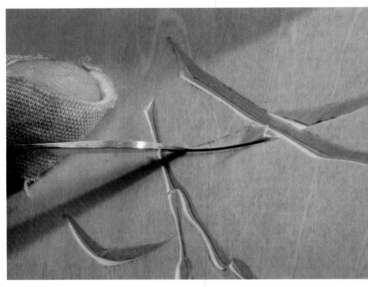

Cut from the stop to the base...

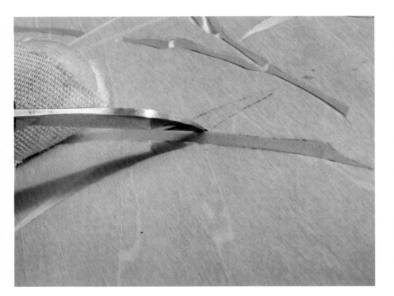

Cut a stop on the other side of the stem.

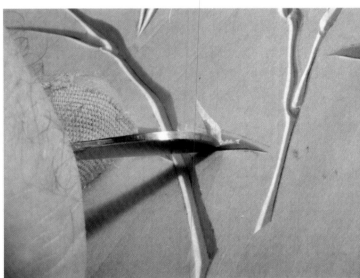

and from the base to the stop, standing the knife up at the end to sever the fibers.

The final result.

Before starting something like the flower blossom I like to think about my last cut. I don't want it to be with the grain, because to the tendency of the grain to pull the knife. With the elements around it already carved, this could be disastrous. I choose to start at the top of the flower, going across the grain. If I work my way around the flower, I will end up with a similar cross grain cut. This petal is basically four sided cut. The first is a short cut from the tip.

The second cut goes to the center. It begins with a plunge to get the knife quickly to the depth I want.

Follow the curve...

Carving
the Black-eyed Susan

The black-eyed Susan involves many of the same techniques used in the previous carving, but the variations may be helpful. By carving one blossom you use all the techniques needed to carve the patterns in this book.

Lay out the pattern on a piece of wood as with the first carving.

and end the cut by standing the knife up to cut the fibers.

ending by lifting up the knife to cut the fibers.

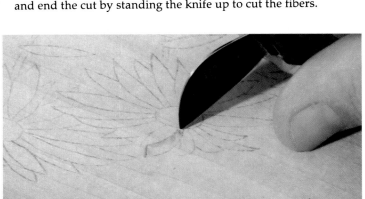

The third cut is a short stop on the perimeter of the flower center. Though it is essentially just a plunge of the knife, these stops around the center create an interesting play of light in the flower.

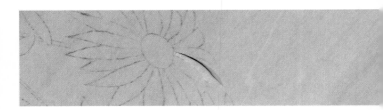

The first petal complete.

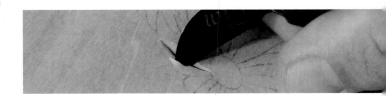

Move to the adjacent petal. You want to cut away from the previously cut, so the first stroke will be along the conjoining side. This is a three cut petal.

The final cut goes from the center out to the tip...

End by lifting the knife up.

Again there is a short stop cut at the flower center.

The third cut goes from the center to the tip.

The result.

The third side emerges from behind the next petal. This creates a crook in the line, but I want to carve it in one stroke for smoothness, turning the knife at the crook.

Some petals appear to overlap. Begin with the adjacent side.

Start shallow so you don't damage the previous petal...

Cut the short stop.

and pivot the blade when you get to the crook.

End by standing the knife to cut the fiber.

When making the stop turn the knife to follow the curve of the center line. With each of these center cuts we are creating an oval center for the flower.

The result.

The next petal has a slightly longer side along the flower center. Begin with the adjacent side creating a ridge.

Return to the point.

Because of the grain direction, I would probably break through the wall if I carved these as I did the other petals. Instead I will treat this as a four-sided cut, starting at the adjacent side.

The ridges are quite delicate, so after I have completed some, I protect them by placing an index card over them on which I rest my hand.

the last petal is the hardest because both adjacent petals are ready carved. I'll do this side first because it starts at the idest point between the two finished petals, making it less tely to break.

Come back along the other ridge.

The stop cut finishes it.

The center of the flower gets its texture and shadow from the stab knife. The light is from above, so the shadow falls around the bottom and sides.

When creating shadow, I don't want all the stab cuts in the same direction, so I change the angle of my knife. Where the shadow is darkest around the edge I use the strongest pressure. As I move toward the light, the cut get progressively lighter. Start at the bottom. Remember, you can always go back and make them bigger, so start easy.

Rotate the knife a little bit and continue with the perimeter, using the same amount of pressure.

Use a little less pressure as you move up. Stagger the cuts slightly so there is not a strong appearance of rows.

As you move into the light, use less pressure on the knife to make smaller cuts.

There are a couple tiny chips approaching the top and along the upper edge the carving stops.

Finished.

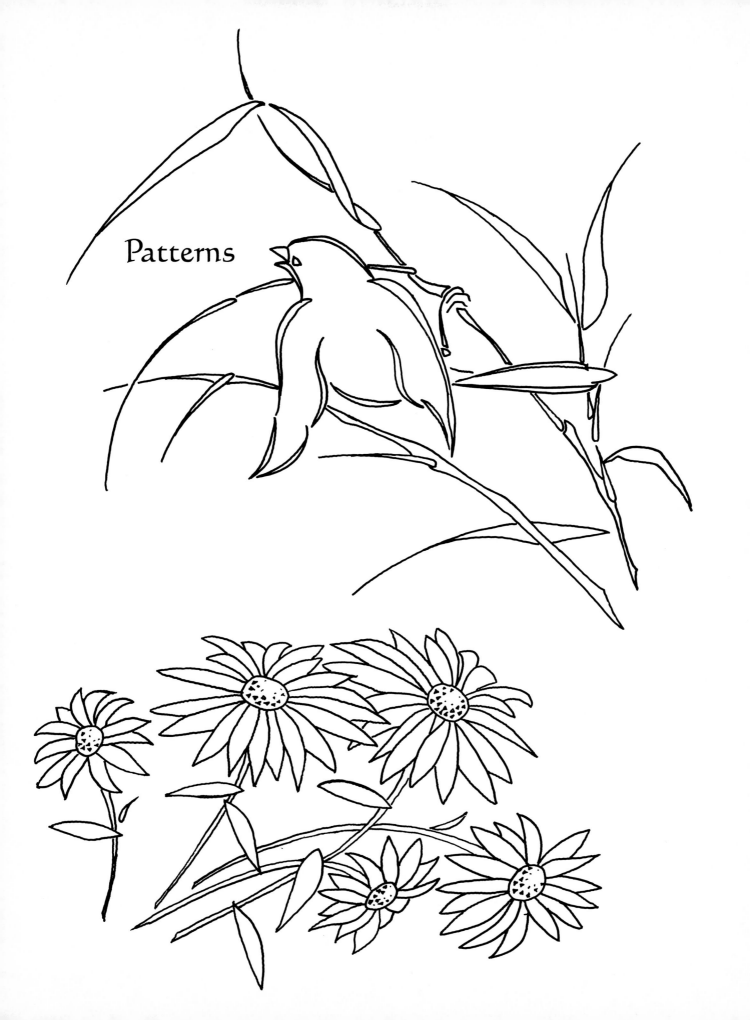

Patterns

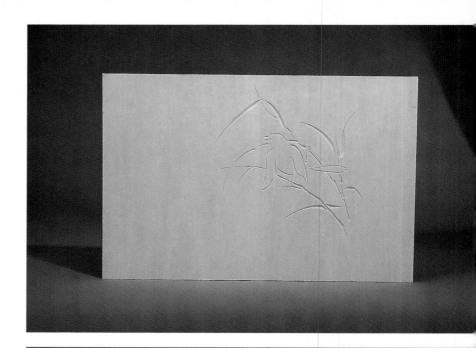

Gallery

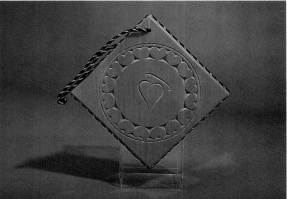